M.B.A. Boot Camp

How to Speak Conversational Accounting

You Can Do This!!

Richard J. Van Ness, Ph.D.
William D. Danko, Ph.D.

For students, graduates, professionals, and all others interested in how the business world works

© 2018
Richard J. Van Ness and William D. Danko

All rights reserved.

Published by MillionDollarPress.com

We do not give specific legal or financial advice: confer with your trusted advisors regarding your circumstances.

Pseudonyms are used to protect the identities of organizations or individuals who have requested confidentiality.

Neither the authors nor the publisher shall be liable or responsible to any person or entity with respect to any loss or incidental or consequential damages caused, or alleged to have been caused, directly or indirectly, by the information contained herein.

You are responsible for your own choices, actions, and results.

ISBN-13: 978-17-23905-74-2

Acknowledgements

I thank the many people who offered input and support throughout this project. I would be remiss in not acknowledging an outstanding group of reviewers for their many valuable contributions that literally shaped the final format and content of this tutorial.

A very special thanks to Raymond K. Van Ness, Ph.D., Robert Brew, M.B.A., M.S., C.P.A., Susan Kauffman, J.D., C.P.A., Ralph Norcio, C.P.A., Ph.D., Edith M. Donohue, Ph.D., and Ira Rosen, C.P.A..

Again, it has been an enjoyable venture bringing yet another book to fruition with my coauthor Bill Danko.

Richard J. Van Ness, Ph.D.

It was a natural progression to collaborate with Rich Van Ness on this project after we published *Richer Than A Millionaire ~ A Pathway To True Prosperity*. In that book, the question of implementation was not adequately explored. After reflecting on my career as an academic and consultant, I know this tutorial would not have been possible without the insights provided by my students and clients.

William D. Danko, Ph.D.

About The Authors

Richard J. Van Ness, Ph.D. is an author, management consultant, and for 28 years, professor of finance, accounting and management. His research includes wealth building and economic sustainability for micro-enterprises. Most recently he coauthored the research-based book *Richer Than A Millionaire ~ A Pathway To True Prosperity*.

William D. Danko, Ph.D. is coauthor of *The Millionaire Next Door*, a research-based book about wealth in America that has been ranked as a bestseller by the New York Times for more than three years. Most recently he coauthored another research-based book: *Richer Than A Millionaire ~ A Pathway To True Prosperity*.

Table of Contents

M.B.A. Boot Camp

HOW TO SPEAK CONVERSATIONAL ACCOUNTING

1. Introduction
2. Frequently Used Terms and Buzz Words
3. Key Financial Reports
4. Journals and Entries
5. General Ledger
6. Debits and Credits
7. T – Accounts
8. Applied Accounting
9. Trial Balance
10. Financial Statements
11. Closure of the Accounting Period
12. How to Prepare the Income Statement
13. How to Prepare the Statement of Owners' Equity
14. How to Prepare the Balance Sheet
15. Select Accounting Forms
16. Thoughts for Next Steps

1. Introduction

The M.B.A. Boot Camp series was written in a non-cluttered succinct format and in plain English. The purpose of this series is to provide insight to those considering earning an M.B.A. degree. For those with an MBA, it will serve as a refresher. For those who just desire an expanded knowledge base of the business world will also benefit. Further, the books in this series are ideal for those with an entrepreneurial spirit and strong interest in starting a business.

We begin with a straightforward discussion of the entire accounting cycle. Next, the "How To's" of financial statement preparation are presented. Lastly, abbreviated forms for record keeping are provided.

Accounting is the language of business and is used as a basis for decision-making. The practice of accounting involves analyzing transactions and converting them into "accounting language" that is expressed in the form of journal entries.

2. Frequently Used Terms and Buzz Words

Accounting speak is a way of expressing the effects of economic transactions of a business or non-profit organization. Accounting is the process of classifying, recording, summarizing, analyzing, and interpreting economic transactions. The major objective is to provide information that is useful for management decisions. Succinctly, accounting tracks:

ITEM	DEFINITION
Net Income	The difference between revenue and expenses
Assets	What is owned
Liabilities	What is owed
Equity	Net worth (Assets minus Liabilities)

It is important that you learn the language of accounting since it is spoken, written, read, and interpreted by entrepreneurs, managers, bankers, suppliers, unions, lawyers, and government agents, among others.

The principle accounting statements are the income statement, balance sheet, statement of owners' equity (or in the case of a corporation a statement of retained earnings) and the statement of cash flows. The balance sheet demonstrates that the total assets are equal to the total of liabilities plus owners' equity. Otherwise expressed, the owners' equity (or net worth) is the sum of assets minus liabilities. The income statement reveals the amount of income (or profit) and is the sum of net revenues (or sales) minus expenses. The statement of owners' equity shows the beginning capital (or equity) balance in addition to any changes throughout the year and provides the ending capital balance. The statement of owners' equity is structured as follows: beginning capital balance + income (or − loss) + additional capital investment − funds withdrawn for owners' personal use. The statement of retained earnings is the equivalent financial statement for a corporation and is structured as follows: beginning balance + after tax income (or − loss) − dividends. The statement of cash flows is a summary of all cash receipts and cash disbursements for a specified period of time. It reveals cash flow from operating, investment, and financing activities.

Financial statements reflect the condition of a business at a particular point in time and are prepared at least once a year.

3. Key Financial Reports

The two key financial reports are the balance sheet and the income statement. Although other reports are prepared, such as the statement of cash flows and the statement of stockholders' equity or statement of retained earnings, they are not as significant as the balance sheet and the income statement.

More specifically, the balance sheet, also known as the statement of financial position, is comprised of the following:

The dollar amount of the assets, debts, and the difference between the two is called net worth or owners' equity.

Or:

Assets minus Liabilities = Owners' Equity

The income statement reveals how much profit or net income has been earned during the period covered by the financial statement, be it a month, quarter, or year. As mentioned earlier, this statement reports revenues (sales), expenses, and the difference, which is known as net income or net loss for the period.

The income statement reports:

Revenue minus Expenses = Net Income or (Net Loss).

4. Journals and Entries

A journal is a place in which business transactions are recorded. It is similar to a diary since financial activity is recorded in chronological order. The journal is called the book of original entry because this is the place where all financial transactions gain entry to the organization's books of record. Most businesses have several types of journals, which are used to record different kinds of transactions. The listing that follows gives a quick review of a selection of transactions and the appropriate journal into which each would be posted.

TRANSACTION	JOURNAL NAME
All cash receipts including payments received from customers	Cash Receipts
All cash payments including payments to creditors	Cash Payments
Purchases of merchandise on account	Purchases
Payrolls issued	Payroll
Sales on account	Sales
Transactions other than those for special journals	General

Transaction data are recorded in the appropriate journals thereby systematically sorting, organizing, and summarizing a variety of transactions so that business activities are able to be quantified and posted into a place called the General Ledger.

5. General Ledger

The general ledger is the place where summarized transactions are stored. There are five major classes of accounts:

TYPE OF ACCOUNT	DEFINITION
Assets	Items owned
Liabilities	Debts
Owners' Equity	Net worth
Revenue	The value of products or services sold
Expenses	Costs incurred related to generating revenues

Amounts are posted from the journals into the general ledger, which serves as a recapitulation of financial transactions on an account-by-account basis. For example, the asset account of cash will receive entries primarily from both the cash receipts and cash payments journals. Cash receipts will increase the value in the account whereas cash payments will have the opposite effect. Occasionally there may be an entry from the general journal to record adjustments to the cash account. At the end of a month or a longer period, each account is totaled and will have either a debit or credit balance. Illustrations of journal entry writing and postings to the general ledger accounts follow the discussion of debits, credits, and "T" accounts.

6. Debits and Credits

The system of double entry accounting requires that whenever there is a debit there must be an offsetting credit or credits. Therefore, there must always be equality between debits and credits. For the books to be in balance every journal entry must affect at least two different ledger accounts and the total of the debits must equal the total of the credits in each transaction. The inventors of accounting decided that debits belong on the left side of the journals and ledgers and that the credits belong on the right side of these two places.

Sample General Journal

	GENERAL JOURNAL		
Date	Accounts	Debit	Credit

Sample T Account as used in the general ledger

GENERAL LEDGER	
Debit	Credit
Account Name	

7. T Accounts

Each business account has its own T account in the general ledger. These places are used to organize and display activities and balances. Depending on the *normal* balance of each account a debit will either increase or decrease its value. For example, asset accounts have a normal balance of debit, so each time the asset account of cash is debited its value will increase and each time it is credited its value will decrease. The opposite is true for accounts that have a normal balance of credit. A listing of normal balances for the five account classifications follows:

ACCOUNT TYPE	NORMAL BALANCE
Assets	Debit
Liabilities	Credit
Owners' Equity	Credit
Revenue	Credit
Expenses	Debit

8. Applied Accounting

The sequence of accounting activities is illustrated with an example. Every item to be accounted for must begin with a transaction. After appropriate treatment of each account, information is summarized and used for preparation of the financial statements.

Sample Flow of Accounting Activity

Transaction →	Documentation →	Journal Entry	Debit	Credit
Buy office supplies for cash	Invoice	Office Supplies	120.00	
		Cash		120.00

Journal entries are posted to the general ledger exactly as indicated in the journal.

General Ledger Accounts

Debit	Credit		Debit	Credit
Office Supplies			Cash	
120.00		(balance) 5,000.00		120.00

An *account* is a separate record where transactions are accumulated. These accounts are kept in a place called the *general ledger*.

Examples of accounts are cash, accounts receivable, office supplies, inventory, accounts payable, notes payable, rent expense, promotional expense, and owners' equity.

The *left side* of the account in the general ledger is the *debit side* and the *right side* of the account is the *credit side*.

GENERAL LEDGER	
Debit	Credit
Account Name	

9. Trial Balance

All of the accounts in the general ledger are totaled at the end of the accounting period and the account titles together with their balances are listed. This listing is called a *trial balance*.

Example of the Trial Balance

Trial Balance

	Debit	Credit
Cash	4,880	
Accounts Receivable	1,950	
Office supplies	120	
Inventory	3,200	
Prepaid Insurance	850	
Land	79,800	
Mortgage Payable		9,000
Accounts Payable		6,500
Notes Payable		2,900
Capital (Owners' Equity)		17,290
Drawing (money for personal use)	8,200	
Sales		84,840
Wages Expense	18,000	
Supplies Expense	80	
Utilities Expense	1,800	
Promotion Expense	1,650	
	120,530	120,530

10. Financial Statements

The Income Statement accounting equation is: Revenue – Expenses = Income. The first accounts listed in the income statement are the revenues (such as sales, fees earned, rent revenue, service charges, and such revenue reduction accounts as sales returns and allowances and sales discounts). Expense accounts are

9

those that report costs incurred in an effort to generate revenues. These accounts include cost of goods sold, selling expenses, and general administrative expenses.

Sample Income Statement

Income Statement

Sales		$ 84,840
Operating Expenses:		
Rent Expense	$ 6,000	
Wages Expense	12,000	
Supplies Expense	80	
Utilities Expense	1,800	
Promotion Expense	<u>1,650</u>	
Total Operating Expenses:		<u>$ 21,530</u>
Income		<u>$ 63,310</u>

The Statement of Owners' Equity reveals the value of assets in excess of liabilities.

Statement of Owners' Equity
Generic Model

Beginning Capital Balance		$
add: Additional capital investment	$	
Income	$	
deduct: Drawing $		
Loss $		
Ending Capital Balance		$

Statement of Owners' Equity

Beginning Capital Balance		$17,290
add: Income	$63,310	
deduct: Drawing	<u>8,200</u>	
Increase in Owners' Equity		<u>$55,110</u>
Ending Capital Balance		<u>$72,400</u>

The Balance Sheet contains assets (items that are owned), liabilities (items that are owed), and owners' equity (the difference between total assets and total liabilities). The Balance Sheet accounting equation is: Assets = Liabilities + Owners' Equity.

Sample Balance Sheet

Balance Sheet

Current Assets		
Cash	$4,880	
Accounts Receivable		1,950
Office Supplies	120	
Inventory	3,200	
Prepaid Insurance	850	
Total Current Assets		$ 11,000
Plant Assets		
Land		79,800
Total Assets		$ 90,800
Current Liabilities		
Accounts Payable	$6,500	
Long Term Liabilities		
Mortgage Payable	9,000	
Notes Payable	2,900	
Total Liabilities		$18,400
Owners' Equity		
Net Worth		$72,400
Total Liabilities and Owners' Equity		$90,800

The statement of cash flows includes the movement of cash among operating, investing, and financing activities. Operating activities include cash receipts and disbursements from business operations. Net cash flow from these activities will usually vary from the net income for the period since revenues and expenses may not be received or paid at the same time that these transactions are journalized. Investing activities include the purchase and disposal of fixed assets such as buildings, equipment, and land. Financing activities include capital investment by owners, debt incurred such as loans, and in the case of sole proprietorships and partnerships, withdrawals of cash by the owners.

A Statement of Cash Flow

Statement of Cash Flows

Cash flow from operating activities:		
Cash received from customers	$82,890	
Less cash paid for expenses and to creditors	<u>15,030</u>	
Net cash flow from operating activities		$67,860
Cash flow from investing activities:		
Cash down payment for land		($72,070)
Cash flow from financing activities:		
Owners capital investment	$17,290	
Less cash withdrew for personal use	<u>8,200</u>	
Net cash flow from financing activities		<u>$ 9,090</u>
Net cash flow and cash balance		<u>$ 4,880</u>

11. Closure of the Accounting Period

The revenue (sales) and expense accounts are *closed* at the end of the accounting period into an account called the *income summary*. The income summary is closed into the capital account and the drawing account (money taken for personal use by the owners) is also closed into the capital account. This process zeros out the balances in the revenue, expense, and drawing accounts so that they may be used for next year's business transactions. The balance sheet accounts are not closed.

The closing entries would be recorded in the general journal and then be posted into the respective general ledger accounts as illustrated below.

General Journal

Closing Entries

			Debit	Credit
12/31/20xx	Sales		$84,840	
	Income Summary			$84,840
12/31/20xx	Income Summary		$21,530	
	Rent Expense			$ 6,000
	Wages Expense			12,000
	Supplies Expense			80
	Utilities Expense			1,800
	Promotion Expense			1,650
12/31/20xx	Income Summary		$63,310	
	Owners' Capital			$63,310
12/31/20xx	Owners' Capital		$ 8,200	
	Owners' Drawing			$ 8,200

General Ledger Accounts

```
      Sales
84,840 | 84,840
      -0-
```

Rent Expense	Wage Expense	Supplies Expense	Utilities Expense
6,000 | *6,000*	12,000 | *12,000*	80 | *80*	1,800 | *1,800*
-0-	-0-	-0-	-0-

Promotion Expense	Income Summary	Owners' Drawing	Owners' Capital
1,650 | *1,650*	21,530 | 84,840	8,200 | *8,200*	8,200 | 17,290
-0-	*63,310* |	-0-	| 63,310
	-0-		| *72,400 balance*

As mentioned earlier, the balance sheet accounts remain open in the general ledger for use in the next accounting period. The account balances remaining open must be listed on a statement and totaled to confirm that debits indeed equal credits. This statement is known as the post closing trial balance.

13

The first day of the new year reversing entries are recorded for the appropriate deferral and accrual entries. Preparation of these entries is beyond the scope of this book, but further discussion may be found in a book on financial accounting theory.

A recapitulation of the accounting flow and sequence of financial statement preparation follows:

Transaction → Document → Journal Entry → Post to General Ledger → Total General Ledger Accounts → Prepare a Trial Balance → Post Adjusting Entries → Prepare an Adjusted Trial Balance → Post Closing Entries → Prepare an Income Statement → Prepare a Statement of Owners' Equity → Prepare a Balance Sheet → Prepare a Statement of Cash Flows → Post Closing Trial Balance → Reversing Entries.

12. How to Prepare the Income Statement

This section presents summary data and demonstrates how to incorporate these data into the income statement. All data for inclusion in the income statement and the balance sheet comes from the adjusted trial balance. The first section of an income statement is the *revenue* (sales) component; it includes the gross amount of sales, deductions from sales, and net sales. The revenue or sales section is generally written as:

```
Sales                                              $
    Less:  Sales returns and allowances     $
           Sales discounts                  $
           Total                                    $
    Net Sales                                      $
```

Sales returns and allowances are included in this financial statement because it reveals the activity of goods being returned. It may be

14

that returns are a result of untimely deliveries or quality problems. Regardless of the reason for return of goods the value of these returns may be easily converted to a percentage of sales. If this percent increases from year to year, or if it is disproportionately high as compared with industry norm, then management must examine the causes of this occurrence and if indeed a problem exists, it must be corrected. The financial statements are essentially reports of management performance and are designed for reading and action by internal business personnel. Of course, the financial statements are required by such outside interested parties as lenders, investors, unions, governmental agencies, and others.

The next section of the income statement is called the *cost of goods sold* or cost of merchandise sold. The activities revealed in this section quantify all costs associated with the process of producing or acquiring products for resale. The cost of goods sold is then subtracted from the net sales to derive an amount known as the *gross profit*. The cost of goods sold section is usually presented as follows:

Cost of Goods Sold
Merchandise Inventory
   January 1, 20xx $
Purchases $
   Less: Purchases returns & allow. $
          Purchases discounts $
Net Purchases $
Transportation-in $
   Cost of goods purchased $
Goods available for sale $
Less ending inventory $
   December 31, 20xx
Cost of Goods Sold $

The *beginning* merchandise inventory is always listed first. This amount is the same as the ending inventory from the prior fiscal year. *Purchases* is an asset account that is debited throughout the year with the amount of goods that are bought for resale or for components that are bought to use in the production of goods that are offered for sale. Any purchases that are defective or in some other way unacceptable and returned to the supplier are credited to an account called *purchases returns and allowances*. This account total at the end of the year is used to reduce purchases since it represents the value of goods not actually kept. *Purchases discounts* are amounts that are subtracted from the purchase invoice in accordance with terms of payment. For example, if the terms of payment are 2% discount if paid in 10 days on a $1,000 purchase, and payment is made within the specified period, then $20 is credited to the purchases discount account. At the end of the fiscal period the total in this account is used to reduce the total amount of purchases. *Net purchases* are derived by subtracting from purchases the total of purchases returns and allowances and purchases discounts. *Transportation-in* is an account that tracks the cost of getting the inventory on site. This cost increases the value of the inventory. The sum of net purchases and transportation-in is added to the beginning inventory and that total reveals the *merchandise available for sale*. From this amount the *ending* inventory is subtracted and thus yields the *cost of goods sold*.

The cost of goods sold is subtracted from net sales and the difference is known as the *gross profit*. The next section of the income statement includes the operating expenses usually described as selling and administrative. Operating expenses are those not directly associated with the cost of production, but rather they are costs required to promote and sell products and for general overhead costs to support the business. A sample operating expenses subsection of the income statement follows:

Operating Expenses
Selling expenses:
    Sales commissions $
    Promotion expense
    Miscellaneous selling expense
    Total selling expenses $

Administrative expenses:
    Office salaries expense $
    Insurance expense
    Rent expense
    Office supplies expense
    Miscellaneous administrative expense
    Total administrative expenses $
Total Operating Expenses $

The *operating* expenses are categorically presented as selling expenses and administrative expenses. *Selling* expenses are those costs directly related to sales efforts. Some are easily defined, such as sales commissions. Other selling costs are somewhat more difficult to allocate, such as executive missionary sales work. In any event, some costs may be allocated to one or more of the business activities. *Administrative* expenses include such costs as office salaries, insurances, computer supplies, office equipment depreciation, and other general office overhead type costs. Both the selling and administrative expenses are added together and subtracted from gross profit to determine operating income.

The final subsection of the income statement includes *other revenue* and *other expenses*. These classifications are for items that are extraordinary to normal business activities. An example of the "other" section follows:

Other revenue
    Interest revenue $
    Rent revenue
    Total other revenue $

Other expense
    Interest expense $
    Loss on sale of plant asset
    Total other expense $

For an example of other revenue, assume that a wheel rim manufacturer has a surplus of cash and temporarily invests it in certificates of deposit that earn $8,000 during the year. Revenue that was earned from this investment has nothing to do with the operation of making wheels. Therefore, it is extraordinary revenue and belongs in the *other* section of the income statement, otherwise the revenues from normal income generating activities would be artificially inflated. The same principle applies to other expenses. If an enterprise sold one of its plant assets at a loss, then the loss incurred is not a part of normal costs of enterprise activities, so it belongs in the other section of the income statement.

The bottom line of the income statement is the *net income before tax*. This figure is the result of subtracting all costs associated with operating expenses from gross profit to derive the amount of *operating income*. The "other" expenses and/or revenues are combined with operating income and this yields net income before tax. It is this amount upon which the tax calculations are based.

Data are presented in the form of an adjusted trial balance and then entered on the appropriate line in accordance with the income statement model. The same data are used for the balance sheet explanation.

Adjusted Trial Balance

	Debit	Credit
Cash	$ 68,500	
Accounts receivable	113,000	
Inventory	180,000	
Prepaid insurance	3,300	
Retail store supplies	1,700	
Office supplies	500	
Store equipment	105,000	
Accumulated depreciation — Store equipment		$ 47,000
Office equipment	60,000	
Accumulated depreciation — Office equipment		22,000
Accounts payable		67,000
Salaries payable		2,800
Unearned rent		500
Note payable		102,000
Owners' equity		215,000
Owners' drawing	35,000	
Sales		999,880
Sales Returns and Allowances	12,500	
Sales Discounts	6,500	
Purchases	635,000	
Purchases Returns and Allowances		9,500
Purchases Discounts		5,500
Transportation-in	6,200	
Sales Salaries Expense	85,845	
Advertising Expense	28,000	
Depreciation Expense — Sales Equipment	9,500	
Store Supplies Expense	2,050	
Miscellaneous Selling Expense	1,335	
Office Salaries Expense	61,000	
Rent Expense	30,000	
Insurance Expense	7,200	
Depreciation Expense — Computer	4,800	
Office Supplies Expense	1,200	
Miscellaneous Administrative Expense	1,650	
Rent Revenue		1,000
Interest Expense	12,400	
Totals	$1,472,180	$1,472,180

It should be noted that only the revenue and expense accounts are used for the income statement, whereas the assets, liabilities, and owners' equity accounts are used for the balance sheet. A link between the income statement and the balance sheet is the statement of owners' equity. This connecting statement follows the income statement.

Income Statement
For Year Ended December 31, 20xx

Revenue (Sales)			$999,880
Less: Sales returns and allowances	$12,500		
Sales discounts	6,500		19,000
Net sales			$980,880
Cost of Goods Sold			
Beginning Inventory — January 1, 20xx		$180,000	
Purchases	$635,000		
Less: Purchases returns and allowances	$9,500		
Purchases discounts	5,500	15,000	
Net Purchases		$620,000	
Add transportation-in		6,200	
Cost of goods purchased		$626,200	
Goods available for sale		$806,200	
Less ending inventory — December 31, 20xx		$225,000	
Cost of goods sold			$581,200
Gross profit			$399,680
Operating expenses:			
Selling expenses:			
Sales salaries expense	$85,845		
Advertising expense	28,000		
Stores supplies expense	2,050		
Depreciation expense — sales equipment	9,500		
Miscellaneous selling expense	1,335		
Total selling expenses		$126,730	
Administrative expenses:			
Office salaries expense	$61,000		
Rent expense	30,000		
Depreciation expense — computer equipment	4,800		
Insurance expense	7,200		
Office supplies expense	1,200		
Miscellaneous administrative expense	1,650		
Total administrative expenses		$105,850	
Total operating expenses			$232,580
Operating Income			$167,100
Other revenue			
Rent revenue		$1,000	
Other expense			
Interest expense		$12,400	$−11,400
Net income before taxes			$155,700

13. How to Prepare the Statement of Owners' Equity

The statement of owners' equity illustrates changes in capital position. It is the connector between the income statement and the balance sheet. A model of this financial statement using data from the adjusted trial balance and the income statement follows:

Statement of Owners' Equity
For year ended December 31, 20xx

Beginning equity (or capital) balance		
January 1, 20xx		$215,000
Income	$155,700	
Drawing	−35,000	
Net change		$120,700
Ending capital balance December 31, 20xx		$335,700

The income is added and if there was any additional capital investment by the owners it too would be added to the beginning equity balance. If there was a loss rather than income then the loss must be subtracted from the beginning balance. Drawing is the amount of cash the owners take out of the business for personal use and this must be subtracted from the beginning equity balance. The sum that remains after all of these considerations is the ending equity or capital balance, which is placed on the balance sheet in the owners' equity section.

14. How to Prepare the Balance Sheet

The balance sheet is a statement that reveals the financial condition of the business at a certain date, which may be the end of the fiscal year or some interim period. Accounts listed on the balance sheet include assets, liabilities, and owners' equity. These accounts are held in balance with the equation: assets = liabilities + owners' equity.

The balance sheet begins with *assets* and these accounts are divided into two categories, *current* assets and *plant* assets. *Current* assets are those that will most likely be used up such as inventory for the manufacturing process and/or those that may be converted into cash (liquidated) within a relatively short period of time (no more than a year). These assets are referred to as being highly liquid and include such accounts as cash, notes receivable, inventory, and prepaid expenses. *Plant* assets are those that generally have an expected useful life of more than one year. These assets usually are depreciated over their expected useful life and include such items as production equipment, office equipment, computers, buildings, and land. Each of these assets may be depreciated, except land. The format for the asset section of the balance sheet follows:

Balance Sheet
December 31, 20xx

Assets
Current assets:
    (likely to be used up, resold, or liquidated within one year) $
    Total current assets $
Plant assets
    (likely to be long lasting and usually require more than a year to be liquidated) $
    Total plant assets $
Total assets $
    (the sum of current and plant assets)

The next section of the balance sheet includes the *liabilities* of the organization. Liabilities are amounts that are owed and are separated into two categories, *current* liabilities and *long-term* liabilities. *Current* liabilities are those that are due within the present fiscal year and include such accounts as accounts payable, salaries payable, and taxes payable. *Long-term* liabilities are those that are due and payable for periods of longer than the current fiscal year and include such accounts as notes payable and mortgages payable.

Liabilities

Current liabilities
    (those accounts that must be paid within the current fiscal year) $
    Total current liabilities $

Long-term liabilities
    (those accounts that are due in periods beyond the current fiscal year) $
    Total long-term liabilities $
Total liabilities $
    (the sum of current liabilities and long-term liabilities)

The last section of the balance sheet is the *owners' equity*. The owners' equity is the excess of the assets over the liabilities. This section also includes a total sum of the liabilities added to the owners' equity. Contingent upon the type of organization formation, the equity section may be referred to as stockholders' equity (in the case of a corporation) or owners' equity (in the case of a sole proprietorship or partnership). The assumption in the illustration of balance sheet preparation is that the organization is a sole proprietorship or a partnership. An example of the owners' equity section follows:

Owners' Equity

Name of owners
    (from the statement of owners' equity) $
Total liabilities and owners' equity $
    (the sum of owners' equity plus total liabilities)

A balance sheet follows.

Balance Sheet
For Year Ended December 31, 20xx

Assets
Current assets:
Cash		$ 68,500	
Accounts receivable		113,000	
Inventory		225,000	
Prepaid insurance		3,300	
Retail store supplies		1,700	
Office supplies		500	
Total current assets		$412,000	
Plant assets:			
Store equipment	$105,000		
Accumulated depreciation	−47,000		
Book value		$ 58,000	
Office equipment	$ 60,000		
Accumulated depreciation	−22,000		
Book value		$ 38,000	
Total plant assets		$ 96,000	
Total assets			$508,000

Liabilities
Current liabilities:
Accounts payable		$ 67,000	
Salaries payable		2,800	
Unearned rent		500	
Total current liabilities			
Long-term liabilities:			
Note payable		102,000	
Total liabilities			$172,300

Owners' Equity
Owners' names:	$335,700
Total liabilities and owners' equity	$508,000

After studying the income statement, the statement of owners' equity, and the balance sheet it should be easy to understand the sequence of the preparation of these financial statements. The income figure is needed to enter into the statement of owners' equity and the ending equity balance is needed to complete the balance sheet.

Preparation of the statement of cash flows would normally follow the other financial statements. However, data are required from the prior year to ascertain increases and decreases in various accounts and such a comprehensive analysis is beyond the scope of this book. The reader may refer to an accounting textbook for an in-depth discussion of the theory and methods to prepare the statement of cash flows.

15. Select Forms for Accounting Records

Special journals are set up to combine similar business transactions. For example, each time cash is received it may be recorded in the cash receipts journal. At the end of a month the journal is totaled and the amounts are posted to the respective general ledger accounts. The post reference column is used in journals to record the movement of data from the journals to the ledgers. The post reference in the ledgers is used to record the source of the data that have been entered into the accounts.

Account titles are included in the headings for the special journals to help guide you to the correct accounts in the general ledger.

General Journal

Date	Accounts	Post Ref.	Debit	Credit

Cash Receipts Journal

						Sundry		
Date	Source	Cash debit	Sales Disc. debit	Accounts Receivables credit	Sales credit	Account Title	Post Ref.	Amount debit

Cash Payments Journal

							Sundry		
Date	Payee	Check No.	Cash credit	Purchases Disc. credit	Accounts Payable debit	Purchases debit	Account Title	Post Ref.	Amount debit

Revenue (Sales) Journal

Date	Account Debited	Post Ref.	Accounts Receivable Debit Revenue (Sales) Credit

Purchases Journal

Date	Account Credited	Post Ref.	Accounts Payable Credit	Supplies Debit	Inventory Debit	Other Accounts Debit

Forms for financial statement preparation follow.

Income Statement

Business Name
Income Statement
For Period Ended: _____

Revenues (Sales)		
Expenses		
Income		

Statement of Owners' Equity

Business Name
Statement of Owners' Equity
For Period Ended: _____

Beginning Capital Balance		

Balance Sheet

Business Name
Balance Sheet
For Period Ended: _____

Assets		Liabilities	
		Owners' Equity	
		Total Liabilities and Owners' Equity	

16. Thoughts For Next Steps

Most transactions of organizations are handled by an accounting software program. However, it is prudent to understand the "what" and the "why" of performance data in real time in order to implement ongoing enterprise improvement.

Given the nature of this subject matter it is unlikely that you breezed through this book as if it was an exciting novel. Just remember… this is a reference book and should be used as such.

Yes, of course you can do this!

www.ingramcontent.com/pod-product-compliance
Lightning Source LLC
Chambersburg PA
CBHW031515210526
45464CB00007B/2926